ISBN: 979-8-9893472-0-9
2023

Library of Congress Number: number here
First paperback edition January 2020.
Photographs by Photographer Tyron
Goodman
Reprinted by permission.
Chubby Chicks Cafe
1401 Little Gloucester Rd.
Blackwood, Nj 08012
chubbychickscafe.com

Recipes From
Chubby Chick

CHUBBY

INTRODUCTION

Okay, so let's first, get into what a Chubby Chick really is. Being a Chubby Chick has nothing to do with weight, (even though I do have a few back rolls) a chubby chick is a woman who is an absolute food lover and a connoisseur of flavors. In order to be a chubby chick, one must have exquisite taste buds and a pallet fit for royalty. Now that we got that out of the way....

Whew Chile, if there is anything I know more than great food, it's the single life! The ups and downs, crazy emotional roller coasters, and excitement of the dating life, The list goes on. I swear dating is stressful and not as easy as it looks. Finding the right person takes time, like finding a great recipe. This book is more than just recipes, it's recipes from a woman's point of view while in a kitchen. Turn some music on, Grab a glass of wine, jump in the kitchen, and let's talk!!!

TABLE OF CONTENTS

DATING MYSELF

Dating myself (self-love day)

Have you ever thought about spoiling yourself? I believe if you want others to treat you like the queen you know you are, you have to be able to do it for yourself. I started something called " Self Love Day" when I quickly learned that the dating pool had some pee in it. I was tired of being asked what my favorite color was, just to find out that yet again, he wasn't "the one". I decided that now is my "soft girl" era and if no one will treat me right I will. after all, I AM THE PRIZE!!

Self love Day is ALLLL about you ladies. This isn't the day to worry about them bad kids, the annoying people at your job, or even what guy is checking for you that day. This day is strictly yours. When you first wake up start your day with gratitude. Make a detailed list of everything you're thankful for, Drink a glass of water, do a light workout, then shower, and don't forget to say your daily affirmations in the mirror and throw on something comfortable but cute. Head to your favorite nail salon and if you are anything like me, I want the works! Manicure, pedicure, and hopefully your eyebrow lady is in today. Because we all know the wrong eyebrow lady can ruin your entire life! Like I said this day is all about you, so make sure you fill your self-love day with all things that make you genuinely happy.

For example getting a facial, massage, picking up fresh flowers or even treating yourself to a solo lunch. If you're super busy like me and having a full free day is damn near impossible, I would deal with my full day, put the kids to bed, do my skincare routine, take a long bath, and light some candles. Learning to make an amazing drink for the days you need to destress can come in a clutch and the following 3 recipes cover every situation. Grab your pretty glasses and lets go!

COCKTAILS

PINK WET MIMOSA

INGREDIENTS

- YOUR FAVORITE CHILLED CHAMPAGNE (IM A PROSECCO GIRL MYSELF)
- COCUNUT MALIBU RUM
- PINK WHITNEY
- EDIBLE PINK GLITTER
- FROZEN DRAGON FRUIT
- TOOTHPICK

INSTRUCTIONS

- This drink is best served chilled so make sure everything is cold

- add about 5 pieces of frozen dragon fruit to your favorite champagne glass

- 1/2 teaspoon of the edible glitter (I get mines from amazon)

- 1 Shot of Malibu

- 1/2 a shot of pink whitney (or a whole shot if we're partying)

- Top your glass with your favorite chilled champagne
- Garnish with a few dragon fruit on a toothpick and enjoy!

THIS IS PERFECT FOR BRUNCH WITH THE GIRLS

PINEAPPLE AMIGOS CON BENEFICIOS

INGREDIENTS

- CASAMIGOS
- GIN
- VODKA
- TRIPLE SEC
- MALIBU RUM
- PINEAPPLE JUICE
- ICE
- PINEAPPLE GARNISH

INSTRUCTIONS

This drink is the one that will definetly get you where you need to be! Stong and sexy is a great way to describe this drink. Its the "Lets get lit" Type of drink so make sure you drink responsibly

- Fill your cup with ice the rim

- add in a 1/2 shot of each,gin, vodka and triple sec

- add a shot of malibu and a shot of casamigos

- Top with pineapple juice

- Garnish with Pineapple and enjoyyyyyyyyy

TROPICAL SUNSET

INGREDIENTS

- PINEAPLLE JUICE
- GRINIDENE
- MALIBU
- FRUIT TO GARNISH

INSTRUCTIONS

- This is the drink thats definetly a crowd pleaser! You can make this for any event! I promise, one sip and you'll feel like your on vacation.

- Fill up your prettiest glass with ice all the way up to the rim,

- Add a once of grenidene

- 3 ounces of malibu, 4 if you really feeling yourself

- Top with pineapple juice

- Garnish with any fruit of your choice

PERFECT FOR A NIGHT ALONE OR A NIGHT WITH SOMEONE SPECIAL.

BACK INTO THE PREY

I decided to get back into the dating scene, but this time it would be on my terms!!!! I found out that being picky isn't necessarily a bad thing and since I didn't get out much, I would let the internet lead the way! I would get the kids out the door make myself a sinfully amazing breakfast and let the swiping begin......

Aht Aht... I never said this online dating thing would be easy girl, but hey you gotta kiss a whole lot of frogs to get to your prince right? Besides, it's all about self-care and feeling good! So have fun! fill your time up and don't focus it all on love!

Spending time with positive women is also a great way to start dating, never know who might have some great tips. I love a good girls' night! Chat, laugh, and eat! Nothing like some girl chat therapy! I love to entertain and have my friends over! What better excuse than brunch! These breakfast recipes are perfect for that morning after or an impressive brunch with your girls

BREAKFAST

They're so much expected of a woman. Magically were supposed to be models, doctors, chefs, and the list goes on. Being a woman on the go isn't easy and you can definitely find yourself eating a lot of fast foods and on-the-go meals. I decided I wanted to create foods that didn't take long to prep but tasted amazing so I could just grab and go... but from home. My lifestyle requires meals that you can whip up very fast. I wanted to come up with a meal that was exactly that. Breakfast was always my favorite meal and there is nothing like a good biscuit baby!

NOT HIS MOMMAS BISCUITS

- BUTTER
- BUTTERMILK
- FLOUR
- BAKING POWDER
- SUGAR
- SALT
- CAN PEACHES
- BLUEBERRIES

INSTRUCTIONS

- All right now!!!!! These should've been called the morning after biscuits but they're most definitely NOT HIS MOMMAS BISCUITS. This is the show-off dish

- Preheat oven to 425

- Grab a mixing bowl and add 2.5 cups of flour, 2 teaspoons of salt,4 teaspoons of baking soda, and 5 teaspoons of sugar mix all ingredients together. DO NOT OVER MIX, LUMPY IS OK

- Add 1/4 cup of blueberries, 1/4 cup of diced peaches

- Add in buttermilk and fold together until it is sticky dough

- Take 1.5 sticks of butter and put them in an 8x8 oven-safe dish, place in the oven until melted

- Add dough, cut up 1/2 stick of butter, and top biscuits

- Cut desired squares into dough

- Bake until beautifully golden

Fried Lobster & Truffle Cheese Grits

This recipe is the one that will have everyone asking "when you are making it again", thank me later lol

INGREDIENTS

- TWO LOBSTER TAILS
- ANDOULIE SAUSAGE
- MIXED COLORED PEPPERS
- SHALLOTS
- HEAVY CREAM
- CHERRY TOMATOES
- QUICK GRITS
- BUTTER
- WHITE TRUFFLE OIL
- SMOKED GOUDA CHEESE
- SALT
- PEPPER
- CORN MEAL
- FLOUR
- EGGS
- OIL
- MINCE GARLIC
- PARMESZEN CHEESE

INSTRUCTIONS

- Start with your quick grits. (follow directions on packaging) boil the water add half a stick of butter. add grits and stir continuously because lord knows grits burns are the worst add the other half stick of butts, add in a cup of heavy cream, 1 tablespoon of salt, and 1 tablespoon of pepper, and add in as much shredded smoked gouda cheese as you like

- In a mixing bowl, add 2 cups of flour and 1 cup of corn meal, season to taste

- Beat eggs in a bowl, cut the lobster in half, long ways, deshell, but keep the tail on. dip lobster in egg, then in the dry mixture, fry in hot oil for about 10 minutes or until golden brown, drain excess oil

- In a frying pan, add oil to lightly cover the bottom of the pan, add 1 chopped shallots,1/4 cup chopped mixed peppers, and 1/2 cup cut-up sausage, let brown
- Slice about 10 cherry tomatoes and add in the pan to blister, add in a tablespoon of minced garlic. add in 2 cups of heavy cream, and 1/2 of parmesan cheese, and turn until it thickens up

- Plate with grits first, your sauce, lobster tail, and then more sauce, garnish with parsley

FRIED FRENCH TOAST

THIS IS ONE OF MY RECIPIES I USE IN MY RESTAURANT, ITS FUN AND TASTE LIKE FUNNEL CAKE

- ALL POURPOSE FLOUR
- POWDERED BUTTERMILK
- BAKING SODA
- BAKING POWDER
- SALT
- SUGAR
- VEGTABLE OIL
- OIL
- BRIOCE BREAD
- BERRIES

INSTRUCTIONS

- Heat vegetable oil in a pan or fryer to 375
- In a mixing bowl (I call this chubby mix), add 4 1/2 all-purpose flour, 3/4 dried buttermilk, 1/3 cup of sugar, 2 tablespoons of baking powder,1 tablespoon of baking soda, 1.5 teaspoons of salt, mix with a fork (you can store this mix for pancakes or waffles also

- Add 2 cups of the mix, to 1.5 cups of water, and add in a few drops of butter extract to elevate the dish

- Cut up thick brioche bread, dip it in the mixture, and fry until golden brown

- You can top it with powdered sugar and berries but if you are a little extra like me, I mix heavy whipping cream and powdered sugar and make icing.

So back again at this dating thing, but this time, it's light and no pressure!

Dating in the beginning is so nerve-wracking for me because I don't have any patience. I wanna go on a vacation for date 3 lol unfortunately we have to learn to relax and enjoy ourselves! Something my aunt has taught me over and over again (because I'm hard-headed) when dating you should just enjoy the company! She's taught me so much over the years!

I finally met a guy and, after about 8 dates, I invited him over, of course, I wanted to flex and the best place for me to do that was in the kitchen! They always say the way to a man's heart is through his stomach! So here is what I like to call, soul-snatcher recipes!!! It's a few dishes that I think all men would love and definitely fit for a king!! The best part of dating is creating memories and these recipes are for the books

BANG BANG SHRIMP PASTA

INSTRUCTIONS

- SHRIMP
- HEAVY CREAM
- GARLIC
- CHERRY TOMATOES
- BUTTER
- SWEET CHILLI SAUCE
- SUN DRIED TOMATOES
- PARMESEAN CHEESE
- OLIVE OIL
- CHUBBY SEASONING
- SALT
- THIN SPAGHETTI

- Boil a pot of water for your pasta, add a tablespoon of salt to your water and a drizzle of olive oil

- When water comes to a boil, add pasta and cook until done

- In a frying pan, add a drizzle of olive oil and 2 tablespoons of butter

- Rinse and clean your shrimp, pat dry, add to the frying pan, brown both sides remove from pan, and set aside

- Chop up shallots, cut cherry tomatoes in half, and chop garlic and add to the pan, cook it down, add in two cups of heavy cream, half a cup of sweet chili, half a cup of parmesan cheese and a 1/4 cup of sundried tomatoes, stir until it thickens up

- Add in pasta, plate, and garnish with cheese and parsley

THIS IS A REALLY QUICK MEAL AND ITS HARD TO MESS UP

BOURBON PEACH HONEY LAMB CHOPS

- LOLLIPOP LAMB CHOPS
- CANNED PEACHES
- HONEY
- YOUR FAVORITE PEACH BOURBON, (MINES IS CROWN ROYAL PEACH)
- GRAPE SEED OIL
- PEACH PRERSERVES

INSTRUCTIONS

- Wash and pat dry your Lollipop lamb chops

- Season with sea salt and pepper

- Heat the frying pan with grapeseed oil covering the bottom

- Sear the cops on both sides, remove them from the pan, and set on the side

- Add in a cup of peach preserves, a cup of peaches, a cup of honey, and 2 cups of bourbon, and cook until simmering.

- Put the lamb back in the pan, and toss

Make is when you decide you want to keep him lol definatly a game changer

STRAWBERRY GRILLED WINGS

INGREDIENTS

- CHICKEN WINGS
- BROWN SUGAR
- SMOKED PAPRIKA
- LEMON PEPPER
- ORANGE PEPPER
- ONION POWDER
- GARLIC PEPPER
- GRAPE SEED OIL
- STRAWBERRY PRESERVES
- HONEY
- BUTTER
- STRAWBERRIES
- HOT SAUCE

INSTRUCTIONS

- Wash your chicken and pat dry

- If you can do this the day before, it will be so much better! if not, it's ok

- Combine the seasoning in a bowl, 1 tablespoon each of brown sugar, smoked paprika, lemon pepper, orange pepper, onion powder, and garlic pepper. and 4 tablespoon of grapeseed oil, season chicken

- Light your grill, after placing the chicken on the grill, you can go inside and start the sauce

- Add in 2 tablespoons of butter, 1 cup of strawberry preserves and 1 cup of honey 1 cup of hot sauce, heat until bubbly

- Once the chicken is beautifully grilled, base it and leave the rest for dipping, prepare for lots of finger licking lol

> This is the perfect thing to make when he is bbqing, its great for game night if you wanna impress his home boys

I loveeeeeee being in a relationship where the man makes you feel comfortable enough to be the woman! Comfortable enough for you to be soft and gentle! Men loves bragging about how well his cooks and will consistently say what you made and how impressive it is! So one day when he is getting ready to watch the game, ask if he has eaten, once he says no, offer to bring him and the guys some food.

At this point you won't disappoint because, if you made the recipes in the book, your man is calling you the superwoman of the kitchen. Just consider these recipes your secret weapon, hey girls gotta do what a girl gotta do. All is fair in love and food.

Being in the arms of a man you love can literally be an out-of-body experience! Being in love literally makes you wanna do any and everything to please them! Nothing like making love and then getting up to cook in the middle of the night. We all love something sweet.

Meeting your new man's family can be so scary! Especially if you have have a momma's boy like my most! You never know how people will perceive you! My aunt always told me to be myself and let the best parts of me shine. When meeting mothers I do just that! I cook since that's where the best part of me shine!

I know some moms think all these young girls can cooK is tacos and shrimp Alfredo. I decided to make a down home meal that would not only impress but also be filling! So I made the mother catcher lol All of these recipes are guaranteed to make his mom smile.

FRIED PEACH COBBLER DONUTS

INGREDIENTS

- VEGTABLE OIL
- CAN PEACHES
- WHITE SUGAR
- BROWN SUGAR
- BANANA EXTRACT
- SALTED CARAMEL
- HONEY
- BUTTER
- YELLOW CAKE MIX
- GLAZED DONUTS
- ALL POURPOSE FLOUR
- DRYED BUTTERMILK
- BAKING SODA
- BAKING POWDER
- SALT
- POWDERED SUGAR

INSTRUCTIONS

- Let's start with the peach cobbler, this is a cheat recipe but it works, and trust me ppl will ask for more

- Take two 16oz can peaches and pour them into a pan. add in 2 cups of white sugar, 1 cup of brown sugar, 1/2 cup of salted caramel, 1/2 cup of honey, a tablespoon of banana extract, 1 tablespoon of butter extract. mix well

- Take a yellow cake. mix and pour all on top (DO NOT MIX) Smooth it out carefully
- Take two sticks of butter and cut it into a bunch of squares, put them on top of the cake mix, and bake at 375 for 40 minutes or until golden brown
- Now for the donuts!!!!!!!

- In a mixing bowl (i call this chubby mix), add 4 1/2 all-purpose flour, 3/4 dried buttermilk, 1/3 cup of sugar, 2 tablespoons of baking powder,1 tablespoon of baking soda, 1.5 teaspoons of salt, mix with a fork(you can store this mix for pancakes or waffles also, take some and mix with water until you get a nice consistency

- Heat oil to 375, take your favorite glaze donuts, dip in the mixture, and fry until golden brown
- scoop out some of that peach cobbler, top the donuts, add some powdered sugar, and just sit back and wait for the OMG

BABYYYYYY!!! THIS IS THE ONE!!!!
YOU CAN BRAG WITH THIS RECIPE

STRAWBERRY BANANA POUND CAKE

INGREDIENTS

- CAKE FLOUR
- BUTTER
- EGGS
- BUTTER, SOFTENED
- GRANULATED SUGAR
- CREAM CHEESE
- BANANA EXTRACT
- STRAWBERRY EXTRASCT
- STRAWBERRY PRESERVE
- STRAWBERRIES
- POWDERED SUGAR

INSTRUCTIONS

Preheat oven to 350

- In your mixing bowl, put in four sticks of butter, whip until smooth, add in 3 cups of sugar and cream for 10 minutes, and add in 4oz of cream cheese

- Put in 6 eggs, one at a time, and add 4 cups of flour, one at a time.

- Put in 2 tablespoons on banana extract and 2 tablespoons of strawberry extract.

- Grease your pan very well and dust with flour, pour in half of the cake mix, do a layer of strawberry preserves, then add the rest of the batter

- Bake at 350. for an hour or until cake is golden brown

- Top with powdered sugar and fresh berries

THIS IS THE RECPIE PEOPLE WILL ASK YOU FOR, FEEL FREE TO DIRECT THEM TO MY BOOK LOL

DESSERT

CHOCOLATE SWEET KISSES

- STRAWBERRY PIE FILLING
- SUNDAE CHOCOLATE FUDGE
- PUFF PASTRY
- POWDER SUGAR
- BUTTER

INSTRUCTIONS

- Preheat oven to 350

- Cut puff pastry into squares of your size,

- Add in fudge and strawberry pie filling

- Fold over

- Base in melted butter

- Bake for 20 mins or until golden brown

- Stop with powdered sugar and fresh strawberries and if you really showing off, add whipped cream

QUICK FAST AND GREAT FOR WHEN YOU NEED SOMETHING LAST MINUTE

WOW, THIS BOOK HAS BEEN KINDA THERAPEUTIC FOR ME. OF COURSE, THIS IS LITERALLY JUST A GLIMPSE OF MY CHAOTIC, BORING, CRAZY CONFUSING DATING LIFE (YES ITS ALL OF THAT) THE RECIPES IN THIS BOOK ARE STRAIGHT FROM MY HEART! I PRAY YOU ENJOY

Chef Keira has always had a passion for food. From peeking in her grandmother's pots to coming up with her own concoctions. Food was her passion but it wasn't the career path she was headed towards.

She joined the Healthcare industry and became a Nurse. Nursing started out fulfilling but that passion for food just couldn't lay dormant. To feed that passion she started by baking cakes at home and selling them. She saw immediate success, selling so many she would make her Nursing paycheck in just days. Making the transition to food service, she decided to dive into her first role with no experience, no money, or guidance. Cakes and Cookies in Williamstown, NJ, was her first learning experience in the hospitality industry.

Unfortunately, it only lasted a year and she was back to nursing. Doing small catering jobs was okay but not fulfilling enough!

The fire was lit with a dream of having her own restaurant and Chubby Chick's Café began to develop. She started taking on more catering jobs and eventually opened a ghost kitchen under a restaurant in Philly. Not getting much attention but doing it her own way was the start she needed. That ended after a year but her determination persisted and she quickly pivoted to doing pop-ups.

With the buzz from Catering jobs and a loyal pop-up following, the first Chubby Chick's Café was opened and within 2 weeks she quickly out-grew that space.

After many mistakes, growing pains, and trial and error she opened her location in Blackwood, NJ, CHUBBY CHICKS CAFE, with more locations coming soon, and her very own syrup and pancake mix available now

WWW.CHUBBYCHCIKSCAFE.COM

Milton Keynes UK
Ingram Content Group UK Ltd.
UKHW052338251123
433238UK00002B/42